How to Stay Depressed
OR Kiss it Good-Bye
Through New Discoveries

Dr. Glenn Richards Robinson

First published by Dog Ear Publishing
4010 W. 86th Street, Ste H
Indianapolis, IN 46268
www.dogearpublishing.net

ISBN: 978-1-4575-1145-5

This book is printed on acid-free paper.

Printed in the United States of America

Celebrate
Life!

Introduction

*D*uring 32 years of doing psychotherapy in private practice I have seen many people struggle with depression, and during those years I've probably learned as much from my patients as they have learned from me.

Whether you're receiving treatment for depression, think you may be depressed, have a family member or friend who is depressed, or have curiosity about it and want to learn more, this book is for you. Think of it as a gift to you – a doctor's bag of tricks, er, treatments, for depression – as well as the latest scientific breakthroughs for treating this debilitating disease.

Each year about 16 million new cases of depression are diagnosed in the United States. According to WebMD, 8%-10% of all women and 4%-5% of all men will experience at least one major depressive episode in their lives. The incidence of depression increases with age, peaking among the elderly, who are three to five times more likely to suffer from it than people in younger age

groups. Depression is not an exclusive club. It does not play favorites. It can – and does – affect everyone: rich and poor, famous and infamous, young and old, male and female.

According to the National Institute of Mental Health, 27 million Americans took medications for depression in 2010. Millions of others found relief through counseling and alternative approaches. These treatments had one thing in common: rarely, if ever, did they yield quick results. Disappointed and frustrated at not getting a quick fix, many depressed people become even more discouraged and depressed and often shop for new therapists, new medications, or new approaches. This makes diagnosis and treatment more challenging.

Because depression can wear many masks and the symptoms can vary widely, it is easy to attribute depression's symptoms to other diseases and other causes.

During my years in private practice, I found many highly effective techniques: some traditional, some that may be considered "new age", and some recent discoveries in neuropsychological, alternative medicine, nutrition, and spirituality.

For the most part, I follow the tenets of Cognitive Behavioral Therapy (CBT), which is now considered to be the most effective approach in treating depression. Cognitive Behavioral Therapy is effective because it focuses on what needs to change in the present, and, how to do it.

You don't need to have an advanced degree (passing grades in middle school will do) to find help from this easy-to-digest guidebook of the modern-day treatment for depression.

Treating any major affliction requires time, energy, and a commitment – on the part of the patient and the health care provider. Fear, lack of information, and social stigma keep many from seeking treatment. What a shame – and what a waste. I'm here to tell you that the journey into wellness – and away from depression – is, for many, a liberating adventure, and a pathway to personal growth and happiness. Or, you can simply ignore me, ignore my advice, and then advise others on "How to Stay Depressed." You'll have to choose.

Dr. Glenn Richards Robinson
Portland, Maine
July 2011

It may be no surprise that depression is listed as the number one problem of our times, but, what is a surprise is that most people know so very little about it. They don't know what it is, where it comes from, what to do about it, or, what new advances have been made in treating it. That might sound like a lot of information to learn about, and obviously, anyone feeling depressed would have difficulty in concentrating on too much, too quickly... so maybe we should start at the very beginning ...

SECRET #1:

DEPRESSION CAN WEAR MANY MASKS

Doctor, I'm told that you have a number of powerful secrets for living a happy and healthy life. Is that really true?

People tell me that, yes.

And they are your own discoveries?

Some are, but most have come from careful observation of what I've seen to be genuinely effective for people, as well as from the latest scientific discoveries that seems to hold promise for the future .

Wow. That's exactly what I'm looking for ! What are these secrets?

Whoa, whoa, hold on a minute (chuckling) . First I'll need to know a little something about you.

But where do I start. It's all so confusing to me. I'm feeling so lost ...

Well, let's just start at the beginning. That's where most things start, you know. Tell me about yourself.

My life is a mess and I'm not sure I can even tell you why.

Uh huh, well, let's talk. What's going on?

I feel crummy. I feel tired most of the time, and down in the dumps, and I can't seem to get unstuck. Sometimes, I feel that life is worthless, hopeless. At other times, I've even had dark thoughts. You know, suicide. And frankly, that scares the hell out of me!

Please tell me more.

Sometimes I have trouble getting out of bed – even on a beautiful day. And what's more upsetting, I don't understand WHY I feel this way. It doesn't make sense. I have a good life – a caring family and work that I like. I'm healthy and have money in the bank. I can't single out anything specific that would make me feel this way, and to make matters worse, I have a lot of pent-up anger, and don't know why. Is this depression? Am I depressed? Or am I a complete loony tune?

Ah, now I get it. You feel lousy but think you shouldn't. Correct? And you can't justify the feeling.

That's exactly it.

This is not unusual. And you are not alone. Let me tell you about a patient I had a few years ago. He, too, thought everything was fine. Then, out of the blue, he told off his boss, lost his job, broke up with his fiancé, and was arrested for road rage. All in a single day! On the surface, it looked like all he needed was a crash course in anger management, right? But it didn't help. Then he started therapy with me. We discovered that he was depressed, and with his depression, anger was a major symptom of that depression – a flashing red light. During our sessions we got to the root of the problem, and, in time, his anger diminished considerably.

Is this common?

Sure. Another patient complained of strong anxiety. She described feeling frightened and overwhelmed every time she left home, although she knew in her head that there was nothing to be afraid of. She was a wreck. She became more and more withdrawn, severing almost all contacts with friends and family. After a while, she wouldn't talk on the phone or answer her e-mails.

So anxiety, too, is a symptom of depression?

Yes, for some people it IS the primary symptom. The problem is that many unpleasant and troubling symptoms are simply manifestations of depression. People often assume that external causes are making them feel tired or sad, or cranky. They don't look within.

What are some other symptoms of depression?

Changes in the ability to get along with others; feelings of hopelessness; irritability; poor concentration and memory; dread; apprehension; pessimism; and especially feelings of guilt, are all common symptoms of depression. Depressive symptoms are not always psychological. Sometimes they're physical: aches and pains (headaches and back pain lead the pack), some allergies, fatigue, sudden weight loss or gain, dizziness, and constipation.

What? Depression can cause constipation? I thought I needed more fiber in my diet.

(Chuckling) Maybe you do.

Go on.

Depression can also cause behavioral problems such as excessive sleeping, insomnia, over-eating, and anorexia.

Whoa, hold on. Depression can cause opposite symptoms from one person to another?

Uh huh. That's why some people fear that they've contracted some new type of disease. Depression can also diminish life-long pleasure; it causes people to lose interest in things they had previously always enjoyed. Things like sports, travel, or sex. Another patient thought Viagra would solve all his problems. But he found that it didn't help. After treatment for depression, his symptoms disappeared and his sex drive returned. The same problem can occur with women. Depression causes many women to lose interest, almost total interest, in sex.

So, no, you are not crazy. And you're not lazy. And you haven't picked up some exotic or unnamed illness. You are simply depressed.

But no one is happy all the time. How can you tell if you're genuinely depressed? For instance, someone coming out of a broken relationship is certainly going to seem depressed. Isn't that normal? So when does a normal feeling become a depressed feeling? How can you tell the difference? And especially, how do you decide if you need professional help?

Let me answer your last question first. You need professional help when your symptoms intrude on your daily life, or on how you want to lead your life. If you had a loss – a spouse, a lover, a good companion, certainly you'd be upset. I would *expect* you to feel sad, angry, irritable – maybe hopeless. Those feelings are appropriate. However, you should feel better after a while. Mother Nature has wonderful healing powers. Problems arise when people get "stuck" and stay stuck over a long period of time. That's a matter for concern. When people are unable to alter the situation, or make positive changes by themselves, then they need to consider professional help.

Another question: How do you find the right professional? Search the Yellow Pages? Google "shrinks"? What?

A good place to begin is with your family physician. Tell the physician that you think you might be depressed and would like a referral to a mental health professional; a psychiatrist, psychologist, social worker, or counselor. It is very important to find a therapist that you are comfortable with. This is a very personal journey. If the first therapist is not a good fit, don't be afraid to shop around. You wouldn't marry someone after one date would you? Shop around. Ask friends and family for recommendations. If you come up empty, check the Yellow Pages or Web for a therapist who specializes in treating depression and anxiety.

But how can I tell which therapist is the right one for me?

Trust your intuition. There is no simple answer. A study conducted at Harvard University a few years ago examined all factors they could possibly imagine that might influence the successful outcome of psychotherapy. For example, the years of training for the therapist, the type of therapy, the number of years in practice, whether they are male or female, the age of the therapist, and so on.

The results were surprising – they suggested that the single most important variable was the therapist's personality and how the therapist and patient related.

You mean successful treatment had little to do with all the other factors?

For the most part, yes. Psychotherapy is a complicated journey. You need a guide who is competent, knowledgeable, and, most important, a good fit. Of course, you need to check into the practitioner's licensing and credentials, but then, trust your intuition – go to one session. Is there a good chemistry? Do you feel comfortable sharing personal stuff with this stranger? Do you like the person? Do you feel comfortable in general? Remember, you are making a significant investment in your future health and happiness. Be certain that you feel in sync with your guide.

If you get negative vibes, don't be afraid to change therapists. Some people want to change, but they cave into feelings of embarrassment. They don't want to hurt the therapist's feelings, but trust me, a therapist will get over it. If the relationship doesn't feel right, go elsewhere. And don't feel you have to explain. Honest. Just find someone else. A seasoned therapist might ask you to come in for a "termination session" to process your decision. This is fairly standard, and maybe a good idea. But then, if the same doubts persist, move on.

PRINCIPLE: In your healing process, you can't afford to compromise.

Now let's take a short test to see how your level of depression might compare to others.

PATIENT HEALTH QUESTIONNAIRE 9

Over the <u>last two weeks,</u> how often have you been bothered by any of the following problems?

0 = Not at all
1 = Several Days
2 = More than half the days
3 = Nearly every day

1. Little interest or pleasure in doing things
2. Feeling down, depressed, or hopeless
3. Trouble falling or staying asleep, or sleeping too much
4. Feeling tired or having little energy
5. Poor appetite or overeating
6. Feeling bad about yourself – or that you are a failure or have let yourself or your family down
7. Trouble concentrating on things, such as reading the newspaper or watching television
8. Moving or speaking so slowly that other people could noticed? Or the opposite – being so fidgety or restless that you have been moving around a lot more than usual
9. Thoughts that you would be better off dead or of hurting yourself in some way

If you checked off <u>any</u> problems, how <u>difficult</u> have these problems made it for you to do your work, take care of things at home, or get along with other people?

Not difficult at all
Somewhat difficult
Very difficult
Extremely difficult

(NOTED, BUT NOT SCORED)

Scoring

Add up all the numbers applied to the examples on the PHQ-9

Not at all = 0;
Several days = 1;
More than half the days = 2;
Nearly every day = 3

Interpretation of Total Score

Total Score:	Depression Severity:
1-4	Minimal depression
5-9	Mild depression
10-14	Moderate depression
15-19	Moderately severe depression
20-27	Severe depression

**THIS TEST CAN BE USED REPEATEDLY
TO EVALUATE YOUR PROGRESS**

SECRET: #2: It's all in your head

IMBALANCES IN BRAIN CHEMISTRY CAUSE DEPRESSION

"Come on. Snap out of it! This depression thing is all in your head. Nothing can be that bad." Has anyone ever said something like that to you? If they have, it might make you feel like a wuss who should take control. "Get over yourself. Get your act together. I'm here to tell you... blah, blah, blah." But YOU know how you feel. If you could simply snap out of it, you would. Keep in mind that when it comes to the subject of you, you are the expert. But having said that, without realizing it, your friends and family may actually be on to something when they said, "Your depression is all in your head." It is! Depression is a condition that occurs when your brain chemistry is out of whack.

**YOU are the expert on yourself.
No one can tell you WHAT to feel or
HOW you should feel.**

Wait a minute. Are you saying that depression, including anger and anxiety, are simply the result of a chemical imbalance in the brain?

A good part is, yes. So before you can begin to control your depression, you may need to understand a little about how the brain works, and how electrical and chemical responses in the brain initiate thoughts, feelings, and emotions. Every feeling, thought, or action requires an interaction between nerve cells, called neurons. The brain has over 100 billion of these neurons.

Did you say 100 billion? C'mon.

Yep. And when they connect to other neurons, they can create over a million billion connections. And they are continuously changing and making new connections. Neurons communicate with one another through chemical bridges called neurotransmitters. Neurotransmissions are produced and stored in the neurons and released when activated. It is these minute chemical molecules that enable electrical impulses to pass through the spaces between the neurons, called synapses. It's an expression similar to how hormones regulate emotional changes in the body, which is also a complex procedure. What I'm describing now is, of course, a simplified version.

You're kidding!

It is these chemicals that are responsible for all of our thoughts, moods, feelings, and emotions. Even for what we call our "positive" emotions. When people fall in love, or make love, they release a neurotransmitter called dopamine. That makes us feel good.

What? Brain chemistry can make people fall in love?

In it's simplest form, yes. Brain chemistry is the key that unlocks all our emotions. But, when these chemicals are out of balance, we experience a myriad of physical and emotional problems.

This is very mind-boggling. What I think I hear you saying is that even small changes in brain chemistry can alter nearly ever aspect of our lives. Is that right?

That is right. And our brain functioning is in constant flux. Every time we have a thought or emotion, perform an activity, or eat certain foods, slight chemical changes take place. But the brain constantly tries to maintain a "ball-park" baseline chemistry. When a deviation from that baseline is too great, we don't feel right; we feel different. And an even bigger problem can occur when we've been depressed over a long period of time.

Why is that?

Because that depressed chemical state may begin to feel like our new baseline. When that happens, depression begins to feel normal. So, it is very important to return this chemical "mix" to its pre-depressed state.

You've certainly got my attention. So depression is simply a low level of one or more of these brain chemicals?

Once again, it's far more complicated than that, but you're on the right track. A depletion of a single chemical can be a major factor in depression, but usually it's a combination of them.

I guess what I'm really asking is this: Is there something I can do to return the right balance to my brain?

Yes, but the remedy is not that simple. It is multifaceted. It includes tangible things, such as certain foods and exercises, as well as emotional variables, such as what you think, and "why" you think, and finally, some behaviors.

Ugh. This is beginning to sound more complicated. Is there a short-cut? Is there a medication I can take to regulate these chemicals?

I wish it were that simple. The issue of medication is complicated too. Medication is particularly helpful when someone needs a "jump start." But medications, in themselves, don't cure depression. They mask it, chemically. A depressed person has to make lifestyle changes to sustain a non-depressed life.

I get it. There's no quick fix. You have to make behavioral changes along with medications. Correct?

That's right. In a perfect world, perhaps just taking a pill would suffice. But because depression is so complex, it requires a range of treatment approaches.

But I've already told you, there are times when I've felt so low I could barely get dressed, let alone make changes in my lifestyle. What could you possibly tell people when they feel that bad?

I would tell them about an important study done in the 1950s in which a researcher, Martin Seligman, shocked healthy dogs with a low-voltage electrical current. After a few shocks, the animals withdrew to an area in their cages where they could avoid the shock. Then they were restrained in such a way that they were unable to avoid the shocks. After more shocks, the animals simply gave up. They became docile and passive. They seemed to resign themselves to the pain. Seligman described them as "depressed". The researchers

then untied the animals, but found something very interesting. Although they could now escape the shocks, the dogs didn't even try. They stayed stuck to where they'd experienced the pain. The researchers then found that they had to drag the dogs off the shock grid to help them avoid the pain.

That's a terrible experiment! Was it really worth it? What did the researchers learn?

They drew an analogy to humans. They suggested that some severely depressed individuals might also have to be "dragged" into helping themselves and avoiding pain... even when it is obvious how to do it.

Dragged into helping themselves? That's a sad commentary.

It is. But it's important to keep in mind that depression is treatable – even though a depressed person might have to be pushed or pulled into good health.

Your brain is the filter through which you perceive *everything* in your life. It must be checked and cleaned periodically.

Starting from the inside, out

I need to talk about my emotions. I think they're way out of control. I feel a lot of pent-up anger towards others, and towards myself as well. And I've felt this way for a long time.

One theory holds that depression is anger turned inward, both appropriate and inappropriate anger.

Inappropriate anger? What's that?

Well, appropriate anger is when you feel more-or-less entitled to it, because of how another person has treated you. The other type is more vague and generalized.

Well, I feel it the most when I'm frustrated, like when someone close to me – a friend, spouse, a co-worker – withholds something I need, or blocks a goal. But that's normal, isn't it?

Yes, that's not usual. I'd be more concerned if you didn't feel some anger in those situations. Anger, especially in relationships, often comes from hurt... hurt from rejections, perceived insults, or misunderstandings.

I see. But what's the relationship between anger and depression? When I'm angry, I usually feel energized, not depressed.

It's not the expression of anger that causes depression, but the repression of it. Anger turned inward can also be a major cause of anxiety.

Anxiety? How?

When you repress anger, either consciously or unconsciously, it's like trying to hold a balloon underwater, or squeezing Jell-O. It's awkward, takes a lot of energy to contain it, and it's almost impossible.

Hmm. And it's that struggle that leads to an unsettled feeling on the inside?

Exactly. It can be even worse when people stifle their feelings because they have a strong need to be liked. They wind up with butterflies; unsettled feelings. You know, if you repress anger, opinions, or feelings long enough, you run the risk of not knowing who you are, or losing your sense of "self".

Some people sacrifice their self-esteem and their identity to be liked. That's a high price to pay.

I feel terrible after I express anger; out-of-control and guilty for having lost my cool. I can't seem to win.

I understand. But an honest and spontaneous expression of who you are is okay. You need not feel bad about it. Think of steam in a pressure cooker. You need to let some escape. The more you express anger, the easier and more natural it comes. And keep in mind that

it's always preferable to say something, *anything*, rather than to keep silent or to deny that you're upset.

And that would help with those angry feelings?

It would a good start. But with one caveat: Don't expect everyone to cave in because you're angry. Anger often begets anger in other people. While I can't promise that expressing yourself will improve a situation, I can promise that it will free up some of your inner feelings. And that's a good thing. So be aware that this has some obvious pitfalls. It takes practice. Some people are so afraid of other people's anger that it prevents them from expressing their own feelings.

I'll need more help with this. Thinking about it makes me nervous.

Being afraid is no reason *not* to do what you *need* to do.

I'm reminded of a time when I was in graduate school studying this very subject. I took a day off and went to the zoo where I watched two tigers sitting quietly side by side. I guess one did something to annoy the other. The annoyed tiger sat up, roared, and swatted the other, who quickly retaliated. After a short time, they settled down with no apparent ill effects. A light bulb went on for me. This was exactly what my professors were trying to each us. A feeling is a feeling. You can't decide whether to have it or not. It's just there.

And the healthiest response is to *become aware of it.*

Express it in a way that is appropriate and proportional to the situation. Then, let go of it.

We can learn a lot from children and animals, can't we?

So, "roar" when you're angry, then let go of it. That makes sense. Can you vent all anger – get it out of your system – that easily? Just let it go?

Unfortunately, no. There was an interesting study in the 1960s. Researchers allowed aggressive kids to express their anger as openly and intensely as they wished by whacking a "shmoo" (a large plastic bounce-back doll). Knock down a shmoo and it pops back. To their surprise, the researchers found that the unlimited expression of aggression only generated more aggression. They concluded that it could not simply be siphoned off, and that it was more therapeutic to express a proportionate amount of anger, then let go of it.

That's interesting. I'll try that. But I know that some people, no matter what I say or do, won't get it. They won't listen, or they'll react by getting angry. Like my boss. When dealing with someone like that, it's a no-win. I won't get anywhere, will I?

Maybe not. But just knowing that you could have expressed your anger, but chose not to, can be beneficial. As long as you made the conscious choice not to react – and it's not a cop out! It's important to realize that you cannot express anger to all people – police, supervisors, government officials, and such. With people who have tangible power over you, you must exercise caution. That's common sense. Your goal in general, however, is the honest and spontaneous expression of emotion, but you need to practice.

Give me an example. Where can I start?

Start by expressing your feelings to people who you don't view as risky. A casual friend, perhaps? Someone you feel safe with. Remember, you're an adult, with an adult lifestyle, and you won't be liked by everyone.

No one is liked by everyone.
And you don't *have* to be!

Keep in mind that learning how to express your feelings appropriately is a skill. It will seem awkward at first, but with practice, it will become easier, more effective, and more natural.

But I'm very sensitive. My feelings are easily hurt. Sometimes I get tongue-tied.

I understand. There is a technique that works well for sensitive people. I call it my "secret word" technique. And I will teach you the magic word only if you promise to use it. It's a single word with tremendous power. The word is "ppfftt." Press your lips together, stick your tongue between your lips and blow hard until your lips and tongue vibrate. It's like a sound that kids make when they're annoyed with something. It comes in handy when something happens that you don't like, or when a person says something irritating. Make that noise. You can do it silently or audibly. It's fun, and you'll be surprised at how quickly you can take back your sense of integrity, your sense of power. It's a powerful technique. Try it!

What's assertiveness training? I've heard a lot about that over the years. Does that help with the expression of anger?

Yes, it sure does. Assertiveness training provides the words; anger is the emotion that powers the words. The goal is to state what you want with clarity and honesty. You don't have to be brutally honest to be assertive, and, you don't even have to be angry. Just make a definitive statement about what you want or don't want. Or, even what you think. The pay-off: the more assertive you become, the less anger you will feel.

You don't have to be angry to be assertive.
Assertiveness may be the best cure for anger.

How can someone work on assertiveness?

There are many excellent books and programs on assertiveness training, but most assertiveness trainings share the same basic principles:
- Rehearse assertive statements before you need them.
- Anticipate situations you will need to be assertive for.
- Support your own progress.
- If you slip, pick yourself up and get back on track.
- Make yourself go back and confront a person who steamrolled over you through their aggression.

Are you telling me to confront an aggressive person or someone who wronged me, and then get assertive? Are you kidding?

Many people confuse "assertive" and "aggressive." Let's clear up that misconception. Aggression is an attack. Assertiveness is respecting yourself, but not at the expense of putting the other person down. Assertive statements are based on mutual respect, but include your opinion, wishes, and your needs.

Let's use an example. Suppose you're in a store, waiting in line and someone cuts in front of you. Then, when the clerk asks who is next, that person steps up. An unassertive person might say nothing, grumble to themselves, or leave in disgust. An aggressive person might chew out both the intrusive person and the clerk, while an assertive person might say, "I believe I was next, I've been waiting here for a while," then step forward.

I have trouble being assertive. When I express my own needs, I feel guilty.

That may reflect something from your past. Some people's needs were not respected or responded to as children. Their parents may have focused on their own needs. If that happened, you might have learned to respond to others while repressing your needs, and that behavior leads to guilty feelings whenever you express your own needs, even as an adult.

Now, that's interesting, and it does describe how I was treated as a child. And I guess that might also explain why, when I get what I need, I feel selfish.

A guilty feeling does NOT always mean you're wrong.

Sure. Especially if you learned that getting what you wanted meant that someone else didn't. That would have made it a choice between their needs versus yours. For a number of reasons, their needs may have seemed more important than yours. If that happened, you may have found that you could avoid feeling guilty only by giving up on yourself. This can be a major underpinning of chronic depression.

There is truth to that, and I can remember feeling angry and critical towards myself as a child, and not understanding why.

You were in a double-bind. Anger is energy. It always seeks a target. As we've already discussed, if you choose to repress anger, it is redirected inward. That triggers self-criticism. And criticism is an indirect way of expressing anger.

Criticism is another way of expressing anger, towards yourself or others.

I have another question. Assuming I am honest with myself, and clear in my assertiveness, what happens if I lock horns with someone, and neither of us gives way. Are we stuck forever? Or, is there something I can do to get unstuck?

There's a very powerful technique I call "apologizing."

Apologizing? What? After all you told me about being assertive and honest?

(Laughing) Hold on, hold on. It's a little more complicated. When you're really stuck and want to get unstuck, you can say, "I'm sorry this has happened," or I'm sorry you feel that way." or "I'm really sorry we can't agree on this." Quite often, that's all the other person needs to hear to let go of an issue. You are **not** admitting fault, and you're not asking the other person to. You are making an honest statement. You feel sorry about the situation and that you feel stuck. It's a simple and effective technique that allows both parties to let go of the issue and move on towards a solution.

Hmmm. That could really work. I will definitely try it.

I hope you can see that you do have choices. You can be sensitive to your own needs as well as sensitive to the needs of others. Remember, you are the expert on yourself. You are the only one who can tell others precisely what is on your mind.

You make it sound simple, and almost fun.

It is simple, and it has the power to make enormous changes in your life and set you free. But it takes courage. Have the courage to be yourself.

If you think angry thoughts,
you'll have an angry life.
If you think depressed thoughts,
you'll have a depressed life.

Getting Started

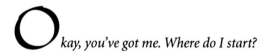

*O*kay, you've got me. Where do I start?

We've already started. You're already becoming aware of your inner feelings, tuning into your full range of emotions, and listening to the part of yourself that feels and is reluctant to feel. Next, have the courage to let those feelings float to the front of your mind. Share these feelings as much as possible because sharing helps validate and clarify your inner emotional experiences. A responsive listener can help you repair the damage done by those who failed to listen.

Is this a plug for a therapist?

(Laughing) No, not really. Any good, patient friend can help. The point of discussing your feelings is to conceptualize the fuzzy notions that float around in your mind. You need to turn them into

clear thoughts, and words. Once you've done that, you can organize, examine, and deal with the thoughts.

Organize my thoughts. I can hardly organize my closet. What do you mean?

Try naming your thoughts. It's a kind of shorthand that will allow you to conceptualize your thoughts. Once they're organized, you can discard or deal with them, as needed. When you tried to organize your closet, I'll bet you earmarked some things for the dumpster, others for charity, and so on.

Go on. I'd like to know more about this.

While you can work internally on the less intense feelings, like poor self-esteem, or insecurity, or low expectations, the more "emotional" feelings, such as anger, guilt, hurt, or grief, need to be expressed. It's important to get them out of the closet, or they'll fester. There is one major exception to this rule, however: talking about depression. Talking ABOUT despair rarely helps the depressed person and, in fact, may make you feel worse.

But depression is my biggest problem. Why shouldn't I talk about it?

SECRET #3:

COGNITIVE BEHAVIORAL-THERAPY IS THE MOST EFFECTIVE TREATMENT FOR DEPRESSION

Because your next step is to begin dealing with it – doing something, not simply venting about it. The style of treatment we'll use is called Cognitive Behavioral Therapy. CBT is highly recommended by the National Institute of Mental Health. It was developed by a therapist named Albert Ellis in the 1950s, and expanded on by Aaron Beck in the 1960s. CBT avoids talking about the emotions, but does focus on the thoughts and behaviors associated with them. CBT was possibly developed out of frustration with the Freudian, or psychoanalytic, approach. You've probably heard about people who were in analysis several times a week and for many years. Well, CBT is designed specifically to be short term and goal oriented. In this therapy an individual examines, revises, and reshapes negative thoughts and beliefs into healthier patterns and expressions.

It sounds like some kind of action-oriented therapy as opposed to a "listening" kind of therapy. Right?

Exactly. Maybe we can begin with an "action plan" right now.

An action plan? Are you kidding? I've already told you – some days I don't have the energy to get out of bed!

I understand. But you need to understand that doing nothing only reinforces depression. Then it becomes a vicious cycle. When

you're stuck you have to break out of it. Remember Dr. Seligman's study with the dogs? Well, the simplest way to begin is to break the pattern and "act as if" you are feeling better.

You mean pretend that I don't feel rotten?

Please do!

Let's say a friend asks you to go to a movie, but you'd rather hang by your thumbs. You can't think of anything worse than going to the movies. Maybe it's one of those down days where you feel exhausted and sad. But make yourself go. Instead of caving in to your depression, "act as if" you're fine, then try to show some interest in the movie. Mention what you like or dislike about the movie, but don't stop there. Make animated facial expressions. Smile often. Straighten your posture. Keep your head up. Breathe deeply, and, of great importance, greet others enthusiastically. In other words, pretend you are enjoying yourself. If you need to, tell yourself you're auditioning for a play. You may even begin to fool yourself.

All you can EVER do is the best you can do.

I thought I was supposed to be honest with my feelings. Now you are telling me to put on an act. What's going on here?

Let me clarify. Once you've recognized that you're depressed, allowing yourself to wallow in it is counter-productive. You'll only feel worse. Depression feeds on itself. Expressing it, or constantly thinking about it, will reinforce it. Acting appropriately will require effort, but it will also start you on your way to recovery.

So, fake it till you make it? Is that it in a nutshell?

Yes. It is actually called the "act as if" technique. It may sound low tech, but it will get you started. And it does work.

Act as if you are the person you want to be.
Your positive feelings will follow.

This technique can also be combined with *therapeutic denial.* The two work very well together.

Therapeutic denial? I've always heard denial was bad. Please explain.

You are in a war! Think of yourself as a soldier and throw everything you've got into the battle! Use all your psychic ammunition. With therapeutic denial, you emphasize your strong points and minimize your weaknesses. Things you can't easily change.

What's the rationale behind this?

If you act like the person you want to become for long enough, you will become that person.

Research indicates that depressed people are much harder on themselves than non-depressed people. They often focus on their faults. They dwell on them. Healthy people do the opposite. They are much more likely to note their weaknesses or mistakes, and then let them go. Let me give you an example of a situation where denial and avoidance can be therapeutic.

Maybe a personal example for me?

Sure. You've said you're a good writer, but a poor speller, right? So you could spend a lot of time tuning up your spelling skills, or simply rely on spell check and focus your energy on your writing skills. You can do that too with personality characteristics!

Work with your strengths.
Don't dwell on your weakness.

That makes sense. And I am beginning to see how all these techniques fit together, but I'm still concerned about how to find the necessary physical energy when I'm at my lowest. You need energy to work on all this stuff.

It sounds like you're assuming that energy and initiative come from somewhere outside of yourself. Trying thinking about your life as something you orchestrate, not just something that happens to you. On a bad day, start with small, manageable steps; steps that move you in the right direction. Try to make each day count for something.

Can you be more specific? When I have a bad day at work – especially on those days when I drag myself to work – is there something I can do that might help?

Yes. Try to increase human contact. Spending time with another person will push you to act less depressed.
- Spend as little time as possible alone in your office.
- Take your coffee and lunch breaks with coworkers.
- "Act as if" you are interested in them as people, not just as colleagues. Ask them questions about their lives (families, hobbies, weekend/vacation plans).
- At lunch, take a walk or visit a nearby gym. Even light exercise can generate energy.

You've given me a lot to think about. And a lot of techniques to learn and implement. I feel a bit overwhelmed.

I know. But also let me offer a caveat. Don't take on too much, too fast. That is setting yourself up for failure. Set realistic goals. Take baby steps. No one succeeds all the time, but everyone needs to try. Even if your effort is only 30% successful, you are still 30% better off.

Success in life is not fate.
It is effort and vision.

So far, we've discussed some simple behavioral techniques to use, but physical changes can also speed your progress

Your Body

- Purposely put on a happy face.
- Smile more often. (It will be reflected back to you.)
- Take care of your body and your appearance. Keep yourself clean, especially your hair.
- Change your clothes often.
- Wear bright colors.

At Home

- Keep your living space clean and neat. Get rid of clutter.
- Pull back the drapes to let sunshine in (natural light is healing).
- Surround yourself with plants or small pets (living things are good company).
- Rearrange the furniture. Repaint the walls with cheerful colors.

Movement

- Be more active. Keep moving. Dance while you vacuum. Play upbeat music and dance by yourself.
- Find the furthest parking spot for your car
- Ride on a swing.
- Choose exercise that fits your age, lifestyle, and physical capabilities. (It is much harder to feel depressed when walking, riding a bicycle, or paddling a kayak.)

Help Others

- Put up a birdhouse and fill it with seed.
- Consider adopting a pet; a dog, cat, or a bird.
- Volunteer to help others, especially in a geriatric or child-care center.

**Although you cannot control what you feel,
you can control what you do.**

Beating Anxiety

I'm trying the things you've recommended and making progress. But I'm having a very difficult time with my anxiety. Sometimes it's so bad, I have panic attacks. My heart pounds, I gasp for breath, I'm light-headed, and my throat tightens. It's not a pretty sight, and it's scary when it happens. I feel out of control.

Anxiety can be a monster. I know that it can be a living hell. Remember my saying that anxiety is a very common symptom of depression? And sometimes the only symptom?

Yes. But why me? And why I do feel I'm afraid when I know there's nothing to be afraid of?

You just said a mouthful. The feeling doesn't match your thoughts. Neurologically, you've fooled your brain into producing the neurotransmitters you would need if you were confronting a dangerous situation.

So, we're back to chemicals in the brain?

Yes. Can you tell me about a recent anxiety attack?

Yes. Saturday, I had to go to the supermarket for a few things. But just thinking about it made me nervous. As I drove to the store, my anxiety grew. When I got there, I could barely function. Not to sound melodramatic, but I felt like I was losing my marbles. I had no reason to be scared. None, yet I went into a total panic.

That's an excellent example. Obviously, you were not afraid of the supermarket or anything associated with it. Except maybe the cost of groceries. That scares me…

(Smiling) I understand that my anxiety was not based on reality, and that's why it doesn't make sense – and why it's so upsetting.

That's the key. Based on your sensory experiences, it doesn't add up. What you are unable to see, however, is the subtle changes in your neurotransmitters. They produce that feeling.

So, I have a short circuit in my brain? Oh boy!

In a manner of speaking, you do. Depression lowers the chemical threshold on what is called the "flight-or-fight" response. This response activates instant energy, but also fear and dread. Neuroscientists call these feelings the "worry circuit."

Boy, if I had a choice, I'd totally eliminate it from my life. How can I do that?

Not so fast! The body is an infinitely complex machine. When confronted with a genuine threat, like a charging lion, the body mobilizes. Within seconds, a large number of very sophisticated responses come together to help the body react. Blood vessels to the outer appendages constrict. Blood flow is redirected toward the brain. Adrenaline surges. Respiration increases, peristalsis in the

stomach decreases, and so on. You're armed to face a potentially life-threatening situation. This self-protecting response is absolutely essential for the survival of the species.

Well, that is impressive, but I haven't faced any lions recently. This "flight-or-fight" stuff is killing me.

The problem is not the response, but that your body overestimates the danger. But the perception is over the top and inappropriate. Your mind is signaling your body to perform unnecessary physical actions. Put another way, it's handing a bazooka to a soldier in combat when there's no battle. The problem here is definitely (but also tangentially) related to your thinking.

Basic anxiety is an overestimated flight-or-fight response.

To treat this type of anxiety, you must reprogram your thinking to more accurately assess the threat of danger. It is not foolproof, but it's a good place to start.

So I consciously decide how much energy I need to fight, or run?

That's right.

What are the triggers for this?

Do you know what most people are afraid of? Other people. It may sound silly, but people with anxiety problems are the most anxious when they are with other people. So, it helps to step outside of yourself and think about how much your sense of "danger" comes from another area; a past experience, or criticism, an old embarrassment, or past difficulties in coping with a failed interaction. When you "hear" those old voices, take note and decide how much anxiety is actually warranted. But do keep in mind that some anxiety is natural. We all feel it.

Can we work with an example?

Suppose you have a chance meeting with an old acquaintance and suddenly become very anxious. Your thoughts, conscious or unconscious, may include: "What does this person think of me?… Am I worthy of her attention?… Do I appear anxious?…" and so on. The irony in this situation is that the other person may be experiencing the same thoughts about you! But, most frequently, the other person is not thinking about you, but rather about themselves. An old proverb says, "A person who worries about what other people think of him wouldn't worry so much if only he knew how seldom they do."

Another test of this theory is to imagine a chance meeting with a child, or mentally challenged person, or a subordinate that works for you. Would you have the same reaction? Probably not.

**People think about themselves
and their own behavior
far more frequently than they think about you.**

(Laughing) You know, I think you're right. I guess we are all a little afraid of what other people think because we usually assume it will be negative. Right?

We all bring pieces of our past into the present. If we didn't, the present would seem unfamiliar and we would have no guide for it. But anyone who is a prisoner of negative memories can become stuck, replaying them over and over. It helps to think about reality this way: No present moment is exactly like what happened in the past. So my advice is stay in the present, stay in the moment. If you do so, you have the power to make today different.

The past does not define the present.
Step out of the past and into your future.

Interesting. Can we review this? Depression causes neurotransmitters to lower the threshold for a "flight-or-flight" response. Worrying about what others think, and blocked or repressed feelings such as anger, can lead to that tense feeling inside. What else do I need to know about anxiety?

Well, there is something else, but you'll need to see your physician. Eliminate all possible physical causes such as hypoglycemia, an under- or over-active thyroid, or hormonal problems. Hypoglycemia is caused by low blood sugar and it can mimic depression and anxiety. And sometimes leads to alcohol abuse.

Alcohol abuse? You're kidding.

Alcohol is made mostly from sugar. Although it can help a person feel normal for a while, the feeling doesn't last.

Can I be tested for blood-sugar problems?

Sure, with a simple blood test. Anyone who is struggling with depression or anxiety and also has a family history of diabetic or pre-diabetic conditions should definitely do this. It is an outpatient test that is highly recommended.

Any other considerations?

Yes, caffeine. Evaluate your caffeine intake. The American Medical Association has called caffeine the "most widely abused drug of our times." Because in low doses it appears harmless, people can easily abuse it without realizing it.

But I love coffee, especially in the morning. I hope you're not suggesting that I give it up.

Let me tell you a little story. A nurse came to me with anxiety problems. As soon as I heard that she worked in a hospital, I pictured the break room during my intern days. There was always a pot of coffee on. When I asked the nurse how much coffee she drank per day she said, "seven or eight cups... but please don't tell me to stop drinking coffee." I told her that she definitely needed to cut down, and suggested that she mix leaded and unleaded (regular and decaf), 50-50. This would immediately cut her caffeine consumption in half. When she returned a week later, after drinking

only 3 cups per day on her new regimen, she said she felt like a new person. Her anxiety had dropped significantly.

What about other foods with caffeine – soft drinks, chocolate, and tea?

They do contribute, but to a lesser degree. Caffeinated coffee is the major culprit. Reduce your caffeine intake and you will reduce anxiety.

Now let's take a short test to see how your level of anxiety might compare to others.

Generalized Anxiety Disorder-7
0 Not at all
1 Several Days
2 More than half the days
3 Nearly every day

Over the <u>last two weeks</u>, how often have you been bothered by any of the following problems? (enter number 0-3)

1. Feeling nervous, anxious, or on edge
2. Not being able to stop or control worrying
3. Worrying too much about different things
4. Trouble relaxing
5. Being so restless that it is hard to sit still
6. Becoming easily annoyed or irritable
7. Feeling afraid as if something awful might happen

Developed by Drs. Robert L. Spitzer, Janet B.W. Williams, Kurt Kroenke and colleagues, with an educational grant from
Pfizer Inc. No permission required to reproduce, translate, display or distribute

<u>Scoring</u>
Add up all the numbers applied to the examples on the GAD-7
Not at all = 0;
Several days = 1;
More than half the days = 2;
Nearly every day = 3

Interpretation of Total Score

Total Score: **Anxiety Severity:**

1-4   Very little anxiety

5-9   Mild anxiety

10-14   Moderate anxiety

15-19   Severe anxiety

**THIS TEST CAN BE USED REPEATEDLY
TO EVALUATE YOUR PROGRESS**

SECRET #4:

YOUR THOUGHTS CAN BLOCK YOUR PROGRESS

What Gets in the Way

I need clarification. You said the brain could chemically rebalance itself. What blocks it from doing so in the first place? How can I help it to rebalance?

That's a very good question. Since we established that your thoughts and feelings brought on your depression, treat it by analyzing those thoughts and reprogramming your thinking. If people make themselves feel bad, they can make themselves feel good. Positive thoughts produce positive changes in the brain.

Do all thoughts produce changes in the brain?

To a degree, but when you continue to think a good (positive) thought or a bad (negative) thought over a substantial period of time, that thought will become a feeling, and feelings lead to changes in brain chemistry. Let's say you think you should have been more successful in life. If you keep reinforcing that thought, it will develop into feelings of low self-esteem. And over a long enough period it will feel normal. Low self-esteem is a significant component of depression.

In the late 1800s a researcher named Stafford required his subjects to wear prism-like glasses for 12 days straight. These glasses made their world appear upside down. The subjects reported being very disoriented; they had trouble with balance, eating, and walking. After a few days, however, they improved dramatically, and learned to function with the glasses on. Within a week the prism view became their new normal. They had become so used to their predicament that they forgot that it wasn't their normal state. This is what can happen with depression.

A persistent thought can become a feeling.
A persistent feeling can make measurable
changes in brain chemistry.

Almost everyone acknowledges that the body and mind are closely connected. Think of grieving, which can alter the body's immune system. It explains why many widowed spouses develop physical illnesses shortly after a loved one dies. Other studies report that many elderly people die immediately after an important milestone such as a birthday or anniversary, but rarely before.

You may have heard the phrase "You are what you eat." Well, I believe "You are what you think" is more important. If dark, pessimistic thoughts and self-doubt fill your mind, they can make you physically ill. The mind is like an old-fashioned tape recorder that plays the same tape over and over. To break out of that endless loop, people need to hear the tape, stop it, and then change it.

You are what you think.
Reprogram your mind to work for you,
not against you.

I'm not sure I can do this. Sometimes sad thoughts overwhelm me and everything I touch seems to go bad. Like the Midas touch in reverse. Maybe I was just born that way.

You weren't born that way. A baby's mind is a clean slate. If your thoughts are frequently negative or pessimistic, it's a sign of a learned behavior. Not something that you inherited.

When people reprogram their minds, they begin to find the optimism and joy we're all born with.

You make it sound easy. But something tells me it isn't.

I didn't say it was easy. I said it was necessary. And there are a number of techniques that can help. Begin to *hear* your thoughts. Pay particular attention to repetitive thoughts that make you feel bad; endless loop tapes. It's not a stretch to see that depressed people expect bad things to happen, which sets them up for - you guessed it -

bad things to happen. You must CATCH and unlearn negative and pessimistic thoughts. The good news: anything you've learned can be unlearned. Even thought patterns.

Any habit you have learned can be unlearned.

There is always something that you can find, no matter how small or insignificant, to support yourself. Learn to look for it.

You know, that sounds a little phony. Do you believe that? I can give you plenty of examples of negative times with nothing positive in them.

Okay, give me one.

This happened to me last year. Although I am terrified of public speaking, I had to make a presentation at work. I prepared well, made slides, graphs, and practiced in front of a mirror for hours. But the presentation did not go well. No one laughed at my jokes. I got anxious and lost my place a few times. It was a poor presentation, and I knew it. You tell me: What was positive about that experience?

A number of things. You mustered up the courage to try something challenging. That took guts. You probably got across at least some of the message, and that was helpful. Your audience probably knew it was hard for you, and respected your effort. But it is *especially* important at times like this to look for positives. *You* need to be your own best support system, and you need to be your own cheerleading section. Many people go through life not learning this. You don't have to be one of them.

Any of your tips for this?

Sure:
- Don't beat yourself up when you slip up; you're only human.
- Catch yourself in the middle of a negative thought; turn it around.
- Cheer yourself on, even with small successes. Especially with difficult situations.
- Appreciate yourself for having the courage to try.

Gaining Momentum

𝓘'm making some progress, but these behaviors are well entrenched. Can you offer any more thoughts on this?

Sure. Be absolutely DETERMINED to attack negative thinking. Then, be vigilant about keeping the negativity at bay. Bad thoughts will try to slip their way into your mind. Don't let them in. You are the gatekeeper. Your job is to banish them. Again. And again. And again. But stopping a negative thought is not enough. That creates a void in your thinking, and you must fill the void with a replacement thought. The good news is, replacement thoughts can also become habits. Also get DETERMINED to look for the positives in everything that happens and in everything you do – regardless of the outcome. And at the very least, give positive thoughts equal time. This simple shift in emphasis can have enormous consequences in changing what you experience.

But most of the time I don't even notice I'm becoming negative.

In Cognitive Behavioral Therapy, that's called "automatic" thinking. Automatic (negative) thoughts just pop into your mind without your awareness. So sensitize yourself to notice any inner-voice thoughts that sound discouraging. Listen carefully and you may recognize the scolding tone as the voice of someone from your past. Even then, it's still a learned voice. Recognize it for what it is. And talk back to it. Then, substitute a supportive voice.

But I can't just turn off negative thinking like a faucet. It's very ingrained. I've probably been this way since I was a child.

That's true. That's what makes this challenging. So it becomes even more important to *attack* your inner critic. And remember, you were not born that way.

Anything else in your bag of tricks to help with this?

Yep. Here are some concrete techniques that might help on your worst days:
- Banish the thoughts by saying "Stop it" or "Shut up" out loud. (Just don't tell anyone that I told you to talk to yourself).
- Wear a rubber band on your wrist and snap it when negative thoughts intrude.
- Picture a red stop light flashing in your mind.
- Touch your forehead and "pull" the negative thoughts from your mind.

All people need to find techniques that work best for them. Keep in mind that it is absolutely essential to silence those old voices and talk back to them. Do so and you'll be surprised at how quickly you regain power over yourself and your life.

It's important to keep in mind that the first thought that pops into your mind does **not** reflect the whole you.

You are not responsible for your first thoughts.

This "automatic thinking" business is tricky. But I'll try it. Anything else that might cue me when I do this?

There's another technique called *labeling*. With labeling, you make up names, even comical names, to describe your thoughts. It's a type of short-hand to raise your awareness of how you think.

For instance, you might label a tendency to expect the worst your "Charlie Brown" thoughts. Your critical voice might be your "Doctor Doom" thoughts.

Yeah, I like that! What about bad things from the past? Things that can't be changed. How can one deal with that? I'm an expert at dwelling on past failures.

The bad news is there is no way to change the past, but here's the good news. The past is done, finished. There is an old story about training elephants that will illustrate my point. If you tie a baby elephant to a post, it will try to get away. After a while, it resigns itself to the fact that it can't escape. Years later, if you take the same elephant, now adult, and tie a rope around the same leg, the elephant won't even try to break away, although it easily could. In other words, the elephant

is trapped by its own memories. Even when the past no longer exists, it can exert a powerful hold on the present, if you allow it.

The past does not exist anymore. What happened even a second ago is gone forever

So you're saying I carry the past into the present by always expecting the worst? You may be right. I even worry in advance. Is there a name for that?

Yes, it's called a tendency to "catastrophize." For example, suppose you are planning a trip to Central America where there are cases of mosquito-born illness. Most people would simply pack insect repellants, avoid infected areas, and go. But people who "catastrophize" would exaggerate the thought until it becomes a full-blown, anxiety-provoking concern. They might fantasize that they'll get sick. Then they'll fret that their inability to speak the language might prevent them from finding a cure, or a way home. You see where this is going? And they might do all that worrying before they even leave home, maybe even canceling the trip.

"Catastrophizing" has no boundaries because it is not based in reality. So solutions are not possible, because the problem has not clearly presented itself. Talk about a no-win situation.

So by reminding yourself that you tend to "catastrophize" you'll remind yourself of your tendency to exaggerate. Then you can remind yourself to keep your thoughts reality based.

Wow! I think this could be helpful. Could a friend or a family member help with this?

Absolutely. People need as much support as they can get. The problem has been years in the making, so the more support you can enlist, the more successful you will be. One woman's husband helped by rolling his eyes and saying, "Wow, that could be a real catastrophe!" whenever she verbalized a far-fetched concern.

But isn't some worry helpful? Maybe a person gets a sense of security knowing he's thought through the worst that can happen, and is prepared for it. What do you think?

Some researcher suggested that approximately 90% of what people worry about never happens.

Ninety percent?

That's right. Or more!

So all the worrying was for nothing?

Worse than that. Worry drains you. It uses up emotional energy that could be better spent elsewhere. Physiologically, worry stresses the body and weakens the immune system.

This seems like an awful lot to work on. I hope I'm not a hopeless case.

Now you've hit something really important that we need to talk about. Hope. Hope is absolutely essential in motivating people to change.

Hope is the magic ingredient in the treatment of depression.

Try this: Close your eyes and picture yourself in as much detail as possible, in an "after" photo. A photo where you look energized, happy, and ready to take on the world. That's a "picture" of hope. Lock that image in your mind then **expect** it to become reality.

Let's take a minute to review what we've covered. You need to *think* about your thinking, and do the following:

- Reset and reprogram your mind.
- Recognize and stop automatic negative thinking.
- Stop "catastrophizing" or making sweeping generalizations.
- Label all unhealthy tendencies.
- Visualize the person you want to be, in vivid detail, and the rest will take care of itself.

Understanding Emotional Addictions

have another issue that I'd like to discuss. It has to do with approval. I'm quite caught up in seeking approval – from almost everyone.

Ah, you're a people pleaser.

Exactly. And I think I've been this way for most of my life. I'm sure that it contributes to my depression. Does people-pleasing also start during childhood? How do I get rid of it?

This is a type of addiction. An emotional addiction is often based on a fear of rejection. And yes, it often comes from something that may have happened during childhood. It's an attempt to influence what others think of you. In essence, it's an attempt to avoid pain.

But I do know, in my head, that it doesn't work. You can't please everybody, all the time. Yet I'm still caught up in trying.

Think about it. If it originated when you were a child, it reflected the logic of, perhaps, a 5-year-old mind.

Now that's interesting. So these childish thoughts may still be influencing me as an adult. What an eye-opener.

But here's the good part. When you think about it now, in the present, you can update the logic to a more appropriate level. Then reset the thoughts that cause you to be such a people pleaser.

I see. The child in me reasoned that if I could keep everybody happy, I would always be liked, and appreciated, and treated well.

Trying to please everyone might have worked for you as a child, but in an adult world, you cannot keep everybody happy without making major sacrifices.

We all want to feel appreciated and needed. When we feel appreciated, the brain even releases a small amount of dopamine. Approval is healthy. It enables us to feel that we're doing a good job of conducting our lives. But if we're addicted to approval – from a spouse, a boss, parent, friend, or even our own children – we've crossed over the line. And that is unhealthy. Perpetual pleasers sacrifice their needs, dreams, and sometimes their lives. Trying to please others all the time is a recipe for disaster.

Well, why don't adult people-pleasers realize this? Why didn't I?

Because you probably became conditioned to looking to other people for your self-esteem. Your primary sense of self-worth might have come from your perception of what others thought about you.

In small measure though, wanting to please others has a good side, doesn't it? How do you know when you've carried it too far, that you've gone beyond being a considerate and thoughtful person?

That's a fair question. Here are some warning signs:
- You do almost anything requested of you.
- You can't say no.
- You often put your own needs and dreams on hold.
- Much of your free time is spent doing things for other people.
- If you do something for yourself and another person does not like it, you feel guilty.

I have to admit, I have to answer "yes" to almost all of these points. I'm pathetic. Where do I go from here?

You are not pathetic. Many people are people-pleasers. But you can choose to leave the pack, get out of the rut, and face the fear. Think about where it originated, and at what age. "All-or-nothing" thinking rarely makes any sense. If someone rejected you when you were, let's say, 5 years old, you may have felt abandoned, and even life threatened. As an adult however, the hurtful feeling of abandonment may be an inconvenience, but not fatal. You have a choice. You are not a child anymore and you should rethink the game plan left over from your childhood.

But, I feel guilty when I focus on myself. It feels like I'm being selfish.

That's common. Do you think you go overboard when you meet your own needs?

Hum. Not really. And I see where you're going with this.

Tolerate the feeling. A feeling is just a feeling. It has no power, and it doesn't necessarily mean you're wrong. Break out of self-defeating behavior and begin to live the rest of your life.

Ooh, boy. That'll make some people unhappy with me.

Maybe, but so what? Feedback can be a way to measure progress. If no one seems to notice the "new" you, you are probably not making progress, and only fooling yourself. No one would willingly give up an accommodating personal assistant, would they? Some people will definitely react when you start asserting yourself. That's okay. Your personal value and sense of self-worth must come from within. You must become your main source of love, support, and approval. Let go of trying to get what you need from others.

Tolerate guilty feelings when you stand up for yourself...

And is praise a similar trap?

The underpinnings are similar, yes. Again, you're seeking your sense of self-worth and self-esteem from others. When you generate praise from within for a job well done, that's different. That's healthy. Looking outside of yourself, even when you do a good job, is precarious.

Precarious? Why do you say that?

Because you are assuming that the person who witnessed your good deed was not preoccupied, sick, or having a bad day. In other words, that person might not have had the ability that day to give you the positive feedback you deserved.

Good point. So relying on others for feedback and praise is always a gamble, huh?

You got it. Go to the head of the class.

If you feel negative on the inside, nothing positive on the outside can have a lasting effect.

But a little praise isn't all bad is it?

Of course not. Praise can be motivating. It becomes a problem only when you crave it. It can become an addiction. Let's take a look at other things that can become addictions, like love or sex. These drives are healthy, normal, and necessary. When a person goes overboard, these drives can become harmful and even destructive.

But isn't the issue how you define "overboard"?

Of course. It isn't a black-or-white situation. There's a wide gray area. If you answer yes to two or more of the following statements, for example, it suggests a problem within the love or sex arena.

- A feeling of loss of emotional control; not conducting your behavior in a way that you think is reasonable.
- Bad consequences; partners that are often angry with you.
- Negative rumors about you.
- Preoccupation with thoughts of love or sex that consume much of your time.
- Living a double life; you are not living the lifestyle you pretend you are.

Are neurotransmitters the culprits here again?

To some degree, yes. Pleasurable behaviors, like love and sex, produce chemical spikes of dopamine and serotonin.

And too much is bad?

I won't go that far, but I can say that pursuing a dopamine "fix" is always disruptive to one's lifestyle. It may work in the short term to make you feel better, but when it becomes an addiction it causes pain.

If the way you live and conduct your life is out of sync with the way most other people conduct their lives, it would usually be defined as a "problem."

So the criterion is based on statistics? Based on other people's behavior?

Yes. Psychological diagnoses are based on statistics. If 95 out of 100 people do a specific behavior in your society, it would undoubtedly be considered "normal." Some societies tolerate behaviors that others do not, like hearing voices. These societies may even value hearing voices as a special or sacred experience.

**Although you cannot control your thoughts
or feelings,
you can control your behavior.**

Peopling Your Life

I'm feeling a little better now. But I'd like to discuss another problem I'm having. I think I'm spending too much time by myself, and it's gotten quite lonely in my cocoon. Yet it's hard to leave. And when I'm with people, I feel anxious and awkward. How did I wind up like this?

It may be helpful to understand why you went into hiding, but just knowing the reason won't automatically fix the problem. Or motivate you to change. Introspection alone is seldom sufficient to initiate change. That's why some people remain stuck. Also, it's a familiar and safe place. When you're alone, you're alone with your own worries, your own self-criticism, and your own doubts. If you decide to change, you risk failure and even success. Both require adjustments. "Peopling" your life is important and necessary for good mental health.

Are you able to help me with this?

Yes, but once again, there is no magic bullet. It's you that has to push yourself to be more socially active. Once again, I'd recommend the "act as if" technique.

Ha, I should have guessed. But at this point, I think I've painted myself into a corner. Won't others think it strange if I start acting differently?

Maybe, but what choice do you have? It needs to happen. Begin with small steps.

B-b-but...

I know it will be uncomfortable at first. Being social is a skill. It will get easier over time, but you must push yourself to make any progress.

Ok. I'll try.

Try to make simple chitchat. Greet people by name, comment on the surroundings, or ask about them. Increase the amount of time you spend with people, especially people who you feel comfortable with. Model your behavior after those who handle social situations well. Surround yourself with positive, upbeat people. And specifically avoid stressful situations, stressful people, or people who are anxious or depressed themselves.

Always work with your strengths.
Do not dwell on your weaknesses.

Doctor, are you suggesting I go to parties? Like cocktail parties?

No, that's too big a step. If you bite off more than you can chew, it will be counterproductive. Begin with simple, short, one-on-one interactions. Choose people that are in your comfort zone. Maybe service people.

I see. So start by chatting with people that I run into every day, like restaurant staff, or a gas station attendant. Say "hi" and make small talk, huh? Then I could move up. Perhaps I could stay and chat in the break room during coffee breaks at work instead of carrying coffee back to my desk.

That's exactly it, good. You've got the idea. Don't be too hard on yourself, but don't be too easy either! Gradually extend the frequency and extent of your contacts. Keep in mind that you are depressed, and you don't want to punish yourself with treatment.

At this rate, I may be an old geezer before I improve. How long will it take?

Let's not worry about that. Once you gain momentum, the pieces will fall into place. And bear in mind, we're not just trying to band-aid your depression, we're also trying to establish anti-depressant techniques that will fortify you for the rest of your life.

**Treating depression is a skill.
Learn it well for a life-long application.**

What about when I really do want to be alone? Is solitude always bad? Should I push myself to avoid it at all costs?

Everyone needs some alone time. But there's a big difference between *being alone* and *loneliness*. One is healthy, the other is not. You have to be watchful when you're depressed. The more time you spend by yourself, the more difficult it will be to rejoin the mainstream. A good rule of thumb is even when you're in a funk, push yourself for some degree of human contact. If not face-to-face, then, at least by phone. Offer a friendly hello and try to smile, even when you're on the phone. Always "act as if" you are up and positive. Remember, feelings are contagious. If you look or sound depressed, others will reflect it back to you, then begin to avoid you.

People tend to reflect moods. If you look or sound depressed, it may be mirrored back to you.

Dig deep for some cheer, even if it's fleeting. People will respond more warmly to you. Studies show that people feel better when they smile. Be aware of your posture, body language, facial expressions, breathing, muscular tension, and finally, your words.

Even failure is evidence that you've tried something.

SECRET #5:

Medications Aren't Magic

This is a lot of work! What about medications? I know you said that there is no magic pill, but what are your thoughts about medications? Might they help me? If so, which would be the most effective?

That's a complex question since there are so many medications used to treat depression. Drug companies have been producing reasonably effective anti-depressants for more than 60 years.

Reasonably effective? That doesn't inspire confidence.

Like I said, there is no magic potion. No hocus-pocus. 1950s drug companies introduced the first somewhat-effective medications for depression. That group, called the tricyclic anti-depressants, included Elavil, Aventyl, Norpramin, Sinquan, and Trofranil. They worked, but not as quickly or effectively as our newer meds. Interestingly, some of the older meds work better for some people than the newer ones. Go figure.

What? Some of the older meds work better than the newer ones?

Yes, for some people they have fewer side effects, and seem to be a better fit.

Can you explain it in terms a 5-year-old can understand? How do they work?

Ok, I'll try. All anti-depressants affect the levels of specific neurotransmitters – serotonin, dopamine or norepinephrine – that influence our moods as well as our perceptions and emotions.

But how do doctors know which neurotransmitters are deficient? Can they measure them?

Ah, there's the problem. You can not measure brain chemistry in a living brain.

So the doctors kill their patients?... Just kidding.

Obviously we'll need to work on your humor a little, too. Doctors prescribe medications based on an estimate of which neurotransmitters are out of whack.

Is that why they often make changes in the medications they prescribe?

Yeah, but sometimes it's also because a patient can't tolerate a specific side effect.

Do most drugs have side effects?

Most do. Some people experience few or no side effects; others experience major problems. The body can tolerate some side effects, not others.

A friend was taking what he called an MAO inhibitor. He had to avoid certain foods. Is that a particularly strong medication?

MAO inhibitors are an older type of medication that can work well for people who are resistant to other treatments. But MAO inhibitors, Parnate, Nardil and Marplan, can interact unfavorably with some foods, like cheese and alcohol. So people taking them have to monitor what they eat.

What about newer medications, like Prozac? I thought Prozac was hailed as the wonder drug.

It can be, for some people. Prozac is included in the SSRI, Selective Serotonin Reuptake Inhibitors, group. As mentioned, serotonin is a major neurotransmitter.

Huh? That's a mouthful. Do I have to remember it?

SSRI will do. Prozac, Paxil, Celexa, to name a few, are all SSRIs.

Do they work the same way in the brain as the MAO inhibitors?

Generally, they do. How they work is more difficult to explain. For some reason this group seems to work faster and focuses on more specific sites or areas of the brain.

Are SSRIs the newest and best meds for depression?

Actually, there's a newer group called SNRIs. That stands for Serotonin-Norepinephrine Reuptake Inhibitor. Effexor, Remeron, and Cymbalta are in this group. Like SSRIs, the SNRIs target specific sites in the brain and influence levels of serotonin and norepinephrine.

This is totally confusing. How would I know which medication to take?

It's your doctor's job to prescribe the medication that most directly addresses your complex of symptoms. For example, if you are extremely anxious, Xanax; if you are sleep-deprived, Elavil might offer a better "fit." Sometimes trial and error may be necessary to match the medication with the patient. Some other medications, such as Trazodone and Ludiomil, block neurotransmitters to help balance the stew.

At what point would a doctor recommend medications for depression?

Good question. It's when a patient appears to be really stuck and needs a jump start. Or when there is a serious chemical imbalance, as in bipolar disorder or suicidal behavior, or when a patient has lost all hope and lacks the energy or motivation to go on. Do you remember the Seligman study? Some people have to be forced into helping themselves. Medication is a way of initiating that process. Then counseling can do its magic.

What's the biggest downside to using medications?

Medications don't cure depression. They are not like antibiotics. They can jump-start your engine, but eventually they have to be discontinued. And they may delay the natural healing process in the brain.

Delay the natural healing process?

Yes. The brain naturally tries to heal itself, if – and that's a big if – people get out of the way. The brain works to produce a state called homeostasis, or balance. Some medications fool the body into thinking it has corrected itself. When that happens, the body begins what neuroscientists call "down-regulating," which slows the body's natural efforts to restore homeostasis. This is especially notable with anti-anxiety medications, and can lead to a "bumpy" feeling.

Bumpy?

Bumpy, yes. Where people appear relaxed but still feel jumpy inside. Anti-depressants and anti-anxiety medications have come a long way, but no medication is able to produce a genuinely natural feeling, and there may be a struggle when patients reduce or try to discontinue use.

Ah, I don't know if I'd want to risk all the side effects.

Anyone taking a medication should know about possible side effects. The bottom line: Those who are debilitated by the depression – or the anxiety - should probably take medication. But don't expect a miracle. Only your body and your mind can heal you.

*That is a lot to digest. Can I review this so that I'm sure I've got it straight? Medications **do** work, especially the new types, but they don't **cure** depression. They modify symptoms by helping the depressed person feel better and gain enough momentum to fight the battle.*

That's it. And when a person is taking medication I stress that they must also make the necessary behavioral and cognitive changes. Relying solely on medications is only postponing the inevitable. Treating depression is multifaceted. Let me say to you again: There is no magic pill. You must un-do what you've done to get into that position.

There is no magic pill for depression.
You must reverse what you've done to get there.

Well, although I do have some very difficult days, I don't think I'm at a totally stuck point, and I would like to avoid taking medication unless it seemed totally necessary. You always seem to have some tricks up your sleeve - er, treatments. Can you suggest any "natural" types of treatment?

Sure...

SECRET #6:

THERE ARE NATURAL PATHS TO HELP HEAL DEPRESSION

Natural Healings

Brand new neurological findings suggest that *how* and *what* we think can help us to reconstitute and **rewire** neurons in our brains. Healthy thoughts can make active changes in the structure of neural pathways.

Just by changing your thinking? It must be a long process. By the way, when we talk about brain chemistry, how many chemicals are we actually talking about?

Although scientists differ on the precise number, there are roughly 50 to 60 brain hormones that have been identified. And when these chemical mixtures, in the synapses, are out of balance, the brain's neurological signal may be weak, distorted, or absent.

I see, so discussing them would be difficult because there are so many.

Yes and no. There are only a few major players that we need to consider.

And they're all effected by what we think? It must be in almost constant change then, huh?

Yes. We've known for some time that brain activity is in constant flux. Recent research has also revealed that diet and exercise can affect brain function. In essence, every time we have a thought or feeling, perform a certain behavior, or eat a specific food, we make minute changes in the brain – electrically, chemically and even structurally. Generally, however, healthy people maintain "baseline" functioning in the brain. When we deviate from that baseline we feel different or not right.

You said there are scores of brain hormones, but probably only a few hitters that we need to discuss. What are their names?

First, you have to understand that neurotransmitters are *endogenous* chemicals. That means they're manufactured in our bodies. Some are classified as excitatory, others are inhibitory, but it's infinitely more complicated than that.

I could have guessed that.

Acetylcholine was the first to be discovered. It is usually excitatory, but not always. It basically effects impulses in muscles, learning centers, short-term memory, and arousal. Based on investigation, it now seems to be less important then the next three however.

Next: serotonin. serotonin is a major player. It seems to produce feelings of optimism, well being, self-esteem, concentration and relaxation. It also effects mood, anxiety, social withdrawal, sleep, and body temperature. Too little serotonin and you may have trouble sleeping, have obsessive-compulsive thoughts or behaviors and, sometimes, violent traits. On the flip side, increasing serotonin will help you relax, produce a sense of well being, and improve concentration.

Then we have dopamine. Dopamine is classified as "inhibitory." It effects arousal levels, libido, pleasure centers, and cognitive functioning. Too little Dopamine may also decrease our ability to learn and remember.

Norepinephrine. Norepinephrine is derived from dopamine. It effects our attention span, anxiety level, arousal, and pleasure centers. Increased levels of dopamine and norepinephrine together can alter energy levels, alertness, speed of thought and muscle coordination.

Okay, I get it. These four hormones cause depression. But how do they get out of whack?

Sorry, again I can't offer a simple answer. There may be many causes. Past history, stress (and how you handle it), genetics, lifestyle, physical changes such as sudden weight loss or gain, diet, and of course your thoughts, can all contribute. The normal aging process can also alter these hormones. So can the long-term use of diet pills, pain pills, narcotics, and recreational drugs. Other culprits can be environmental toxins like pesticides, fertilizers, cleaning products and industrial solvents. Stimulants and depressants – large amounts of caffeine, nicotine, or alcohol – may also come into play. Too much or too little sleep and acute stress can upset the stasis. And, because our brain chemistry creates our thoughts, feelings, understandings, and memories…, deficiencies or surpluses in even a single neurotransmitter can make unpredictable changes. When more than one neurotransmitter is involved, it gets more complicated.

How can I influence my brain chemistry? You mentioned food choices. Can you be more specific? Is this something I can do? If

*neurotransmitters can't be measured in a living brain, how could I
possibly know what foods may be contributing to my depression?*

Although, unfortunately, we can only guess, the predominant
symptom of your depression may offer some clues as to which neurotransmitter may need attention. It often comes down to trial and
error. Try one approach, and if it doesn't work, try another.

It's safe to say, however, that low levels of serotonin are probably
the most common cause of depression.

*Ok. Let's start there. If serotonin is a major player, how can I boost
it through diet?*

Eat foods that are rich in carbohydrates.

Like regular sugar?

No. Sugar won't help. Cells burn sugar very rapidly. So, your serotonin level might spike quickly, but plunge just as rapidly. And that
would make you feel uneasy and shaky. Long-term, slow-burning carbohydrates, like brown rice, corn, whole wheat bread, squash, root
vegetables, fruit juices and whole grains, would be effective. Slow-flow
carbohydrates produce a steadier increase of serotonin.

What else?

Dairy products. But a mix of proteins and carbohydrates are
good, but less effective. Because the high protein content of milk
and cheese lessens serotonin's effect. So, large quantities of dairy
products are not as effective as carbohydrates.

Sounds like serotonin is the big kahuna of neurotransmitters. Right?

I wish I could reduce it to such a simple statement. In matters of the brain it's always more complicated. Let's say that normal and slightly elevated levels of serotonin are related to feeling positive and joyful.

You said that exercise can also influence the production of serotonin.

Yes, but we're talking about low-level exercise such as walking, bicycling, stretching, low-impact aerobics, and dancing.

I see. And what about the other neurotransmitters? Can I increase their levels by what I eat?

Foods that are rich in protein – fish, red meat, chicken, and eggs – increase dopamine and norepinephrine. Especially fish that is high in protein and low in fat like haddock, flounder, or codfish. Skinless white meat chicken and low-fat turkey can also be beneficial.

So avoid fat. Is that what you're saying?

Yes. Fat reduces blood circulation and blood flow to the brain.

Helloooo! Avoid fat.

Yes, an exception is milk, however. Milk is a mixed bag.

Anything else to add?

Eat beans, vegetables, and tofu. They help produce dopamine and norepinephrine. Avoid large amounts of caffeine. As mentioned earlier, if you love coffee, mix caffeinated and decaffeinated – to reduce your intake.

Hmmm. What about exercise? Are there specific types of exercise that might help with dopamine production?

Yes, there are. Here it's the more aerobic exercises – jogging, competitive sports, basketball and tennis, that are recommended (provided you're in good shape and your physician gives you a green light).

I've never been very athletic. In fact, I'm a klutz.

That's okay, you don't have to be a jock. All forms of physical exercise are beneficial. And that includes sex!

Now you're talking!

People who get very little or no exercise have three times the incidence of depression as those who exercise regularly. Exercise also increases the release of endorphins, the body's natural painkillers.

I see. I'll start moving and grooving right away.

Now let's take a look at what happens when you eat poorly – a nutritionally poor diet, which includes refined foods that are high in sugar, additives, and pesticides. Advertisements would have us to believe that some additives are helpful, when the opposite is true. Artificial sugar substitutes for example. In large doses they have been shown to alter brain chemistry in laboratory animals and induce seizures. And wheat protein has been shown to accelerate depression in some people. Hey, I'm not making this up.

Some over-the-counter drugs, such as antihistamines, anti-inflammatories, anti-hypertensives, birth control pills, and some tranquilizers, can lead to depression in some individuals.

And finally, when considering your health, don't pooh-pooh the importance of rest and sleep.

Oh, that's a problem for me. I do have trouble falling asleep and/or staying asleep. I've noticed that when I'm not rested, I feel more depressed. Is this common?

It is. Sleep deprivation causes fatigue, and problems with concentration and memory. New research suggests that it can also influence your judgment and contribute to misplaced confidence.

Ah, like thinking you're right, knowing you're not, but refusing to budge?

Well put. We form and reform neural pathways when we're awake, and thinking, but also when we are asleep and dreaming.

How could scientists possibly know something like that?

By using instruments that perform "position-emission topography" and "functional magnetic resonance imagery."

Ugh. I don't speak that language.

The terminology's not important, but the results are. Researchers at MIT trained rats to follow a maze. Then they implanted electrodes in the hippocampus, a part of the rat's brain. That enabled the researchers to observe patterns of neural firings as the rats ran the maze. Then the scientists observed the rats' "thoughts" when they were asleep, and found striking similarities.

So it appeared as if the rats were dreaming about running through the maze while asleep?

Yes. Humans also have thoughts and memories that operate under our radar screen, and we're not always conscious of these thoughts. Many therapists believe that people work out some day-time issues while dreaming.

I read some Freud in a psych class years ago. Sounds like this ties in with his theories about dreaming, and its importance, huh?

It does. The most famous of the dream theorists, Freud, felt that we disguise the true nature of our dreams to keep us from waking and allow us to continue processing. The next step in sleep research may be to see if humans repeat certain neural firing patterns at night during these "disguised" dreams.

It's well known that depression can alter both REM (dream sleep) and non-REM (close to dreamlike) sleep.

That's interesting, but I'm not sure what it all means.

At this point, it's simply an observation. The ramifications are being investigated. The obvious message is that you don't get a breather from depression even when you're asleep. The problem with sleep studies is that subjective reports can vary with the subject's age and medications.

Medications? Do some medications affect our dreaming?

Apparently so. The older anti-depressants seem to reduce REM sleep; the newer ones seem to have less of an effect.

Once again, I need to remind you of the complexities of studying the brain. The different stages of sleep are identified by different EEG, or brain waves. We cycle through all or most of the stages four to six times per night. They can also differ in length. So, researchers must use caution when interpreting sleep data. The bottom line: There appears to be a close relationship between sleep, dreaming, and our emotional health.

**Proper sleep is absolutely essential
to a feeling of well being.**

You said that there was some interesting new research on ways to treat depression. Like new medications.

SECRET #7:

THERE ARE NEW TREATMENTS BEING DEVELOPED FOR TREATMENT-RESISTANT DEPRESSION

There is research on entirely new types of medications, yes. For nearly twenty-five years, the so-called "new" medications were variations of those previously established. Research today is examining new chemical approaches and new categories or classifications of medication that will work differently in the brain.

Are any of these available to the general public yet?

Not yet, but I expect you will hear about them soon.

What about new approaches other than medications? Are they making any progress?

Yes. A psychiatrist, Helen Mayberg at Emery University is experimenting with a technique she calls Deep Brain Stimulation (DBS). With this technique, an ultra thin electrode is surgically implanted in an area of the brain she calls "area 25." When a low voltage electrical current is passed through the electrode, many of her patients have shown marked improvement. This work is still considered to be in its embryonic state however. But some clinics now are already using what is called "vagus nerve stimulation" for treatment-resistant depression. With it, a small pulse generator (similar to a pacemaker) is implanted in the chest and connected to the vagus nerve.

A low-voltage electrical stimulus to the nerve has produced significant improvement in some people.

Interesting. But is there anything less intrusive?

Yes. There's another new technique in use now called "transcranial magnetic stimulation." It's an external device that creates a magnetic field in the areas of the brain associated with depression.

These techniques are currently being used?

Though still in their infancy, they are gaining traction.

That's impressive. But what about entirely non-medical approaches to treat depression? Are there any alternatives that you would recommend?

Yes. There are a number of totally alternative approaches that can help.

MEDITATION AS A HEALING APPROACH

Have you ever tried meditation?

Meditation? Ugh. You mean finding a personal guru? And sitting for hours like a 3-ring pretzel and chanting "ohmmm?"

(Laughing) No. Hardly. It's not as cult-like as all that, but it does require commitment and discipline.

I'm listening.

When I was interning at Boston City Hospital, in the mid-1970s, there was a lot of hoopla about TM (transcendental meditation). At lunch one day I met Herb Benson, a psychiatrist who was doing research on meditation. He had a hard time swallowing the claims of transcendental meditation without objective research. A thorough and dedicated researcher, he was committed to doing an honest and fair study. I sensed that he probably expected to disprove TM's claims, but I also sensed that he would be professional in his study. When I met him again about a year later, I was surprised to hear his findings.

And?

He said that many of the trappings of meditation – having a guru, enrolling in a long-term training program, or utilizing special space – were quite unnecessary. But he also found that meditation, in its simplest and purest form, was remarkably beneficial. A few years later, he wrote the best seller *The Relaxation Response*, which is still in print today. When I told him I would buy the book, he told me that all I really needed to know was how to meditate.

And he found a special way to do it?

On the contrary. He found there were numerous ways to meditate, and most of them worked, but the key to successful meditation was discipline and determination. You need to do it twice a day, and over a significant period of time.

For how long? Like forever? I have a job and family.

(Chuckling) No, it's not that extreme. And it's not an all-or-nothing proposition. You may begin to see some improvements rather quickly.

Well, we've talked about brain chemistry, electric impulses, sleep patterns and such. What is actually happening inside of the brain when you meditate?

Meditation produces a more restful state of mind that rarely occurs elsewhere during our daily lives. In a non-meditative state, our thoughts run continuously. We go from one thought to another to another. William James, an American philosopher and psychologist, called our thought process "a stream of consciousness."

Wait a sec. Doesn't sleep provide this restful state?

Nope. Sleep doesn't produce a totally restful brain state.

And meditation does?

One of meditation's goals – and rewards – is entering a "non-thinking" state. Imagine your brain as a TV with the volume on high. When you're truly meditating, the TV is off. Is there a challenge in reaching this state? Yes, it's very difficult to stop yourself from thinking. Even at first, when you begin meditating and you have thoughts like, "is this working?" or "wow, I'm really meditating now", you are still thinking. Not meditating. With time, patience, and commitment, most people can find that restful state. Those that do describe it as blissful and restorative.

There is also some evidence, as measured by an EEG, that long-term meditators are able to alter their brain waves to some degree when they are in a fully awakened state. They say they feel peaceful, have improved concentration, and are anxiety-free. Many report few, if any, signs of stress.

Dr. Benson found that the type of meditation did not matter, as long as the person was conscientious and consistent about doing it.

So it's not hard to learn? You don't need special classes?

Correct. There are many excellent how-to books and DVDs. Some people prefer the discipline of a class, but that's a personal choice, not a necessity.

What about a mantra? Do you need a personal mantra to meditate properly?

No, but many people incorporate a mantra into their meditation. It helps them to focus and to relax.

Can you tell this beginner the ABCs of meditating?

Sure.
- Wear loose-fitting clothing.
- Turn off your phone(s), TV, DVD player, and anything else that might interrupt your solitude. Choose a place that is quiet, where you won't be disturbed. After a while you will learn how to tune-out noise. Honest.
- Do some stretches to limber up your body, then sit comfortably (in a chair, on a mat or rug).

- Put your hands in your lap, palms up, and your feet parallel to the ground.
- Keep your back reasonably straight; don't slouch, but don't be rigid
- Close your eyes. Focus on your breathing.
- Breathe slowly and deeply. Don't force your breath. Let it come naturally.
- Choose a word or phrase as your mantra. It can be made up, meaningless and nonsensical, or as simple as "breathe," "peace," or "one." Say it softly and slowly. Say it over and over, and over again. Doing this helps to quiet the chattering of your brain. Soon the internal noise ceases. If your attention drifts, as it will, gently bring it back to focus on your mantra.

And that's it?

That's it. Expect your mind to wander at times, but don't let that bother you. Be gentle with yourself.

Try to meditate for 20 minutes at least twice per day. When you finish the session, slowly open your eyes, stand up, and stretch. Then, try to carry that relaxed feeling with you for as long as you can.

It sounds easy.

It is – and it isn't. The procedure is easy, but it takes discipline. Your mind will wander frequently.

Isn't it boring?

If you find yourself thinking, "this is boring..." you are not meditating, you are thinking! Some days it will flow easily, and some days it may seem almost impossible. Persistence and continuity make the difference. Just as in dieting!

And it will help to lessen anxiety?

It will. One can see brain-wave changes with an EEG, lowered blood pressure, and better concentration.

Sounds like it's definitely worth trying. Is there specific research supporting the benefits of meditating?

I found three studies to be particularly interesting. In the 1990s, Frederick Gage, a neuroscientist, demonstrated how, through meditative techniques, new cells could be encouraged to grow and modify in the hippocampus (the learning, memory, and emotional area of the brain). Before Gage, it was widely believed that it was not possible to grow new brain cells. More recently, at Howard University, Kisband Doirdson tested long-term Buddhist meditators and found heightened electrical activity in the pre-frontal cortex of their brains, an area associated with positive emotions. A third researcher, Sara Lazar, at Massachusetts General Hospital, studied the functional MRIs of long-term meditators, and found that certain areas of the brain (associated with sensory processing and attention) were "thicker" than those of non-meditative groups.

Interesting. And sounds easy. I'll try it. Are there any other alternatives to medicine that might help?

Yes, one's own spirituality.

Spirituality as a Natural Healer

You mentioned that one's spirituality can have a healing effect, and that caught my attention. I do have a strong faith, but I admit to not being much of a participant. Do you honestly think one's religious beliefs can help treat their depression?

Although scientific study of spirituality is relatively new, we've all heard anecdotal stories about miraculous mental and physical healings, attributable to one's religious beliefs. In the Bible, faith healed lepers, restored vision to the blind, enabled the lame to walk, and so on.

In Lourdes, France, as recently as 2005, it was reported that a 90-year-old woman was totally healed of cardiac and respiratory problems, and began to walk after years of immobility. When a team of doctors were asked to examine her, they reported that her healings were "inexplicable."

Ah, we've all heard those stories, I think everyone has. But has science actually studied this type of result?

In 2004, Dr. Jeffery Levin, of Eastern Virginia University, and David Larson, from the National Institute for Health Care Research, documented over 200 cases in which they felt a person's physical healing appeared to be directly related to the strength of their faith or religious beliefs. In 1995, a study at the Dartmouth Medical Center reported that surgical heart patients who described themselves as religious were three times more likely to survive their surgeries than non-religious patients. And in 1996, a research team at the Deaconess Hospital in Boston reported that patients who claimed to feel a presence of a higher power had significantly better health and recovery rates than non-religious patients.

Hey, you're beginning to sound like a "holy roller."

I don't mean to sound preachy. I'm simply reporting research that seems to demonstrate the importance of one's spirituality to their health. In fact, this thinking has become so prevalent that the curriculum of two-thirds of all medical schools now includes a course entitled "Alternative Treatments in Basic Medicine."

But is it possible to do tangible scientific research on faith? How could one do that?

With the advent of brain scans and functional MRIs. With these instruments, Andrew Newberg, at the University of Pennsylvania, found a section of the brain (prefrontal cortex) that is neurologically quite active in religious people, while being only minimally active in those who reported having very little faith. When interviewed about their lives, the "religious" group used words such as "optimistic, hopeful, grounded," and "secure" to describe themselves. They rarely felt lonely. The non-religious or atheistic group reported more pessimism, discouragement, loneliness, and less hope.

Are you saying researchers discovered a part of the brain that is dedicated to religious beliefs?

Trying to make assumptions and interpretations about the human brain is always difficult, but I'll go out on a limb and say that from this study, it does appear that human beings are "hardwired" to believe in something outside of themselves; a higher power. And those with more neural activity in that area seemed to have a better prognosis in most afflictions, including depression.

Did a particular religion or belief system play a part? Did it matter what they believed?

No. The research described what they thought to be a "religious, spiritual, or faith-based" area of the brain. As long as the individual believed in some external supreme being or life force, there was significant neural activity in that part of the brain.

That is very interesting. Can I benefit from this research? Is there a way I could use my own spirituality for self-healing?

Sure. But first you need to comprehend something very basic about one's faith. Eighty percent of our population claims to be "spiritual," while, in fact, there is a big difference between claiming to be spiritual and actually utilizing it.

So I'd have to go to some regular religious service...

No, that's not what I'm saying. *Religion* refers to a specific set of beliefs, instructions, history, "shoulds and shouldn'ts," judgments, and usually guidance for the hereafter. What I'm describing is basic to ALL religions: it's faith. You have to put **faith** into it. It's not enough to merely give "lip service" to your faith. You need to get into it with both feet. Only then will you begin to see results. Who knows? Maybe, a miracle. But you have to *expect* that your higher power *wants* you to be happy. Then you need to *expect* that the universe will comfort and provide for you.

This sounds very "new agey." Bring out the crystals and tarot, and let's sing "Kumbaya."

You can call it "new age" if you like, but I'm just reporting what I've seen work for people. Faith and spirituality have a healing energy that certainly can at least aid in treatment of depression.

You make it sound so attractive, but I was brought up to believe in a punishing and judgmental God. I was always fearful of God's wrath. If I didn't do exactly what I was told, there would be hell to pay! And I was taught that I couldn't hide anything from God. While on the flip side, I was also taught that God loved me very much, and I've always had a problem reconciling the two. I was certain that I could never live up to God's high standards. It scared me as a child, and maybe even scares me a little now.

I understand. It would be hard to love a higher power that you also feared.

Exactly. And the messages we're taught can be confusing. Once when I was in Sunday school, many years ago, my friend Stevie asked the minister what heaven would be like.

"Would there be ice cream in heaven?" he asked. "Pizza? Sports and games to play?"

"No," the minister said, "in heaven we just sit and listen to God!" Stevie was crushed.

"For how long?" he asked.

"Forever!" the minister replied enthusiastically. Stevie was horrified. He turned away with the most horrified look on his face. He couldn't even listen to his favorite teacher for more than a half hour without getting bored. You know, I sometimes feel a little like Stevie. Some things make sense, some don't. What should I believe?

I can't answer that. I'm not here to preach a particular religion or faith. That's a highly personal matter. You might start by simply developing a personal relationship with your God, as you understand him, and you may begin to notice positive changes.

Go on, please.

Then trust your intuition. Pray. Pray for direction in your spiritual quest. Accept the guidance you receive if it seems to come from the heart. Put aside your old fear of punishment. Focus on God as all-loving, and all-healing. Be open to receiving this love, accept the notion that God would want the very best for you. You are his creation – he designed you.

But he knows all my faults, all the crummy things I've done and bad thoughts I've had.

Well, my own feelings are that you haven't surprised God. He is a benevolent god, and *wants* us to celebrate life. Just like we want for our own children.

You know, this is beginning to make sense, and I think those thoughts have healing properties all by themselves. But what about diseases? Accidents? Famines? Genocide? Those horrible things. How can you explain them?

I can't. I don't know. All I can say is that it's been my observation that it's people, not God, that cause most afflictions.

I imagine you're right. But this sounds too simple and too easy.

It is simple, but it's not easy. It requires a genuine commitment. If you have a back-up plan in the back of your mind, you are not putting faith in your faith.

If you make room for your faith your god will step in

Hmmm. How can I make my faith stronger on a day-to-day basis?

I don't know, maybe talk to God. Talk to Him frequently. Talk to him as if he were your best friend.

Do you honestly think that faith can provide inner healing for depression?

Well, let's examine it from a purely psychological perspective. A strong faith allows you to wipe your personal slate clean. It can also free you from feeling all alone. And finally, it can help you to feel that the responsibility for your recovery is not on you alone… you have teamed up with the most loving, accepting, and powerful force in the universe. A force that *wants* you to be happy, and wants you to find joy in your life.

I must admit, this does make some sense. I'm feeling optimistic already.

Fine Tuning

I think you're pretty much underway now, but there are a few more things I need to emphasize. I'd recommend changing your **behavior** first, because thoughts and feelings have lives of their own. And old ways of thinking and feeling die hard. But – here's the good news – by changing your behavior you may see progress immediately.

Remember, you're not starting from scratch. We're not reinventing the wheel. Focus on things you like about yourself. Your ultimate goal is to develop self-love and acceptance. If you continue to feel impatient or critical toward yourself, you will stay stuck. Progress will elude you. Only a "self" that feels embraced and accepted can grow, change, and blossom.

Ah, but loving myself has always been a problem for me. I need to change lots of things.

I understand. But don't expect to change all aspects of your personality. And that's okay. Nobody's perfect and nobody needs to be perfect. Let me repeat that: Nobody *needs* to be perfect. And you will find when you begin to forgive your flaws, those flaws will seem less important. And some of your imperfections will seem less troublesome.

And, as you open yourself to life, to more feelings and to more people, you will create new experiences and interactions. You may even find yourself changing in ways you never expected.

So maybe I'll get more than I bargained for?

Yes. But a caveat… "just say NO" to judgment of your progress, either from yourself or others. Judgment can stop you dead in your tracks. It's another intrusive and unhelpful "voice." Another bad habit from the past. Turn a deaf ear to judgment. Just do the best you can do.

That'll be hard, I've always been self-judgmental.

Then attack it! You are in a war. Unchecked judgment will cause you to give others power over you. This is important: When you judge or criticize yourself, you surrender your personal power.

Personal power? Are we back to new-agey stuff? What do you mean personal power?

Personal power is your self-esteem, your will, your integrity, and your sense of self-worth. Once you have it, no one can take it away… unless you allow it!

Now that's an interesting concept. When I feel unworthy, insecure, or insignificant around other people, you think it's a sign that I've given away this personal power?

Absolutely! You're giving other people more power over you than they have a right to have, or expect. It's up to you to assume the full power of adulthood. It's out there, readily available, but you need to *claim* it – and you need to keep it.

Personal power cannot be taken away without one's permission.

We all want approval from the important people in our lives. But we cannot give up our personal power to gain that approval. When we listen to a critical voice from the past, or we allow self-criticism to gain a foothold, we give away our personal power.

Any time you realize that you've given away personal power, *take it back.*

We've covered a lot of ground, haven't we?

We have. I hope you can absorb a lot of what we've discussed.

It all seems quite logical. It all makes sense to me. It might take me a little time, but I'm on it. Is that it?

Just about, but I've saved what is possibly the most important advice for last.

And that is?

Build yourself a personal "cheerleading section." Create an inner voice that is both a friend and a support. One that will forgive you when you need it, and love you when you feel alone. An inner voice that would say only what a loving and conscientious parent might say. It's never too late to re-parent yourself. Timing is everything. Be the parent to yourself that you've always wanted.

**It is never too late to re-parent yourself.
This time, do it right.**

Now that's a tall order after so many years. Give me some guidelines, please.

- Wipe the slate clean; give yourself a new opportunity in life.
- Say loving and protective words to yourself; the words that you always needed to hear.
- **Promise** yourself that you will stop punishing yourself.
- Protect yourself from outside criticism or mistreatment.
- Let negative comments roll off your back. Don't absorb them.
- Stay away from people who cause you pain, including family, if necessary.
- Seek out people who recognize and accept you for the person you are.

**Spend time with people who make you feel
good about yourself.
Stay away from people who don't.**

I get it. It's up to me to support and protect myself. But doesn't everyone, at some time, need support from other people?

No one can do it alone. Human beings are social animals. But, at this point, you'll need a lot of accepting voices to counter the harsh voices from your past. And remember, friendly voices make a difference only if you can absorb their message. You have the power; you have the choice!

I never thought about it like that. I like this "personal power" stuff.

I can promise you this: If you support and reassure yourself, and accept encouragement from people who wish you well, you will be well on your way to feeling better, and defeating your depression.

You will have created an inner support system that is not contingent upon the whims of others. And this is precisely the armament we all need to carry us through life's most difficult times.

The only person who can truly defeat you… is you. The only person who can truly make you happy… is you.

I'm reminded of an old man I used to pass while driving to my office. He was lying in a hospital bed next to a window of his house. He had snowy white hair and a sad expression. He would look at me with great longing as I drove by in my convertible. We never exchanged any words, but I imagined him thinking "Boy, if I only could take one more walk through the park, or smell the flowers, or watch children playing near the duck pond." He helped me realize that I could still do all these things, and more. And that I should live every day to the fullest, and appreciate the simplest things in life. Because, we could all be like that old man some day, alone and almost immobile, gazing out a window.

Take a walk in the park today!
Celebrate life, every day!

Beginning Your New Life

I'm feeling much better now, Doctor. I have new insight, new techniques, rekindled faith, and real hope for the future. Some aspects of my game plan seem like hard work, but some of it feels almost like fun. I suspect that it will take a while.

It does sound like you're on the right track. And, yes, it will take a while. But you will begin to experience some benefits almost immediately. Be steady, patient, and confident that the changes will occur. Keep in mind that you are trying to change behavioral and thought patterns that have existed for many years - maybe over your entire lifetime. Be firm with yourself, but also kind, supportive, and understanding. Expect relapses and slips; everybody has them. Don't exaggerate or dwell on them, just get back on track as soon as you can. And put energy and thought into becoming the person that you really want to be. Recovery is within your grasp. Remember, even a diamond requires polishing to sparkle.

Celebrate yourself.
Celebrate your life.

I'm feeling quite optimistic about my future now. Thank you, Doctor. We've covered a lot of turf, but I do have to ask… What would happen if I didn't accept your advice? Or chose not to follow it? Then what?

Then what you've also learned is… how to stay depressed!

How to stay depressed? Hey, that would be a great title for a book, wouldn't it?

I don't know… maybe.

Be yourself.
Everyone else is already taken.
-Oscar Wilde

APPENDIX OF PRINCIPLES

(In no particular order)

-Write out and save for quick reference-

- - - - -

How we communicate with ourselves is what
determines what we will truly experience in life.

- - - - -

Always treat yourself at least as well
as you would treat a total stranger.

- - - - -

Assessing blame is neither important nor necessary.
It doesn't help.

- - - - -

All you can ever do is the best you can do.
Let it go at that.

- - - - -

Happiness is not a place.
It's a journey.

- - - - -

Prayer is not to overcome God's reluctance;
it's to request His willingness.

- - - - -

For your faith to be real,
you must put faith in your faith!

- - - - -

Your perception of an experience
is colored by the meaning you assign to it.

- - - - -

Although we cannot control what we think or feel,
we can control what we do.

- - - - -

Ignore judgment.
All you can do is the best you can do.

- - - - -

Our sense of personal power cannot be taken
without our permission.

- - - - -

As soon as you realize you have given away your
"personal power," take it back.

- - - - -

It is never too late to re-parent yourself.
This time do it right.

- - - - -

Spend time with people who help you feel good
about yourself. Stay away from people who don't.

- - - - -

The only person that can truly defeat you... is you.

- - - - -

Happiness must be practiced.

- - - - -

Even a diamond is a polished piece of coal.

- - - - -

You become old only when regrets
take the place of dreams.

- - - - -

Life is a celebration.
Celebrate yourself.

- - - - -

Depression can wear different masks.

- - - - -

A single candle can pierce the darkest night.

- - - - -

75% of all prescriptions for anti-depressant medications
are prescribed in the United States.

- - - - -

A persistent thought can become a feeling.
A persistent feeling can make chemical changes
in the body.

- - - - -

Learn to manage your mind.
Program it to work for you, not against you.

- - - - -

Reconciliation with the present
cannot begin with a defense of the past.

- - - - -

Children often blame themselves to avoid feeling
betrayed and unloved by their parents.

- - - - -

Success in life is not fate.
It is effort and vision.

- - - - -

Beliefs and attitudes color perceptions.
Our perceptions shape our behavior.

- - - - -

When depressed, you are not
perceiving reality clearly.
You are looking into a mirror of your mood.

- - - - -

If you believe you can't escape, then you won't.
If you believe you can, then you will.

- - - - -

The flowers of tomorrow
begin with the seeds of today.

- - - - -

We see things not as they are, but as *we* are.

- - - - -

A friend is a gift for you.

- - - - -

If you feel negative on the inside,
very little positive from the outside
can make a lasting effect.

- - - - -

You were not born with habits.

- - - - -

Any habit you've learned
can be unlearned.

- - - - -

Program your mind for success, not failure…
happiness, not depression.

- - - - -

The past does not exist anymore.
What happened even a second ago
is gone forever.

- - - - -

You can remain a prisoner of your past…
if you allow it.

- - - - -

Learn to view life as something you create,
not just something that happens to you.

- - - - -

Act as if you are the person you want to be.
Your feelings will fill in behind that behavior.

- - - - -

Work with your strengths.
Don't dwell on your weakness.

- - - - -

Criticism is another way of expressing anger,
either toward yourself or others.

- - - - -

Adults with their own lives to lead
cannot keep everyone happy.
Accept that fact.

- - - - -

You are not responsible for your first thought.

- - - - -

You don't have to be angry to be assertive.
Assertiveness is often the best cure for anger.

- - - - -

A guilty feeling does not always mean you're wrong.

- - - - -

You are the expert on yourself.

- - - - -

JUST BE NICE

CPSIA information can be obtained at www.ICGtesting.com
Printed in the USA
LVOW10s2108300713

345434LV00003B/11/P